Where Do P

by Chi Winwood

Orlando   Boston   Dallas   Chicago   San Diego

Visit *The Learning Site!*

www.harcourtschool.com

ISBN 0-15-325484-X

16 17 18 19 20 985 10 09 08 07

Ordering Options
ISBN 0-15-325468-8 (Collection)
ISBN 0-15-326562-0 (package of 5))

Pigs play in a pen.
They like to slip and slide.

Ducks play too.
Where do ducks play?

They play in a pond.
They swim and dive and splash.

4

Rabbits like to play.
Where do they play?

Rabbits hop and hide
in the tall grass.

Do monkeys like to play?

Yes. They play in trees.
They like to jump and swing.